What is a

Are you a Christian?

I was brought up in a Christian home.

That doesn't make you a Christian.

My mother always went to Church.

That doesn't make you a Christian.

I believe in doing good, helping others.

Quite right, too, but so do most people. That doesn't make you a Christian.

I believe in God.

Most people say this, but that doesn't make you a Christian. Many people think they are Christians but rarely bother about Jesus Christ.

Well, what is a Christian, then?

Let's begin at the very beginning....

In the beginning...

when God made human beings, he made them perfect and good and sinless. He wanted us to be his friends and look after the earth.

God did not make people robots or machines. He gave us a precious gift, free will, to choose between right and wrong, good and bad. He did not want to force us to love him. He wanted us to love him freely.

But people chose to disobey God; they chose wrong. They preferred to please themselves rather than God. They sinned. And so sin entered into the world. It is a disease we all have, because **'all have sinned'** (Romans 3:23).

What sin is

Evil, wrong and sin are there in the life of everyone born into the world. We see this in all the hatred and violence, greed and selfishness in the world. We see it as we look at our own lives, if we are really honest with ourselves. It is a part of our very nature. I sin when I come short of God's standard. **'All have sinned and fall short of the glory of God.'**

If the pass mark for an exam is 50 and you get 49 marks, you have failed. If someone else gets 5 marks, he has failed too. It is no good you saying, 'I did much better than the one who got 5.'

50

You have both failed.

49

5

You may think you are not so bad, better than most. But that's not the point, for not one of us has come anywhere near God's perfect standard – Jesus Christ. We can't even come up to our own standards. We may not have done anything especially wicked. We are sinners because we are just not good enough.

I sin when I do what I want. The Bible says, **'Each of us has turned to his own way'** (Isaiah 53:6).

Doing what I want: this is the cause of our trouble, unhappiness and quarrels.

Sin is not just killing, stealing, or telling lies. I sin when I live to please myself rather than God.

I sin when I can't be bothered with God or with other people; when I say 'I'm my own boss; it's my life; I can do what I like with it' – this is SIN – I in the middle – me first.

I sin when I do not love God with all my heart. Jesus said, **'You shall love the Lord your God with all your heart and with all your soul and with all your mind. This is the first and greatest commandment'** (Matthew 22:37-38).

Not one of us has loved God like this. We have all broken the great commandment. We are all self-centred rather than God-centred.

6

What sin does

Sin spoils
Sin is like an ugly blot on a clean page. Being selfish, lazy, thoughtless, telling lies and dirty stories ruins your character. Sin destroys the happiness of a home and friendship.

Sin spreads
Sin is like weeds in a garden; if not rooted out, they will soon overrun it. Little acts of dishonesty and disobedience soon become habits we cannot break.

Sin separates
Sin is like a thick cloud which blots out the sun. That is why God seems miles away. He is pure and holy. He hates sin. He cannot and will not look at sin. It blocks the way to him. Sin cuts you off from God in this life and in the life to come. Be quite clear about this; hell is a grim and dreadful reality for all who reject Jesus Christ in this life.

What are you going to do about it? You cannot remove the barrier. You cannot save yourself. Trying to help others and doing good cannot remove this barrier either. If sin results in our being cut off from God, is there no hope for us? Has God washed his hands of us?

Why Jesus came

God is love. He proved his love for us, by sending Jesus into our world – fully human and fully God. **'God so loved the world that He gave his only Son, that whoever believes in him should not perish but have eternal life'** (John 3:16). Jesus did not come just to show us what God is like and live a perfect life. He came to remove the barrier between us and God.

God's character is like a coin with two sides: justice and love. His justice rightly condemns us, for sin must be punished. His love makes him long for us to become his friends again. On the cross, his justice and his love were perfectly satisfied. Sin had to be punished, so God in his love sent his Son, Jesus Christ, to die in our place, bearing the death penalty our sins deserved.

That is why he cried from the cross,

My God, my God why have you forsaken me?

The full punishment for our sin was taken by Jesus. As a man once put it, 'He carried the can for everybody.' Jesus suffered 'the agony of being cut off from his Father for us.'

Just before he died, Jesus said, **'It is finished!'** This was not a cry of defeat, 'I've had it!' No, it was a cry of victory, 'I've done it! The debt of man's sin is paid.' The way back to God is now open.

His work of saving you from hell and eternal destruction is finished. The barrier of sin has been blasted away. Jesus died for us, his body was put in the tomb and a great stone pushed across the entrance. But he rose from the grave – he is alive. He won the victory over sin and death.

The way to God is now wide open.

Do you want to live an easy-going, 'do-as-you-like' life? Do you want to remain dissatisfied and only know the empty, passing pleasures of the world? Then don't read any further. Carry on just as you are; don't bother about Christ.

But remember this: one day you will realise too late that you have missed the best in life, wasted your life and ruined your own soul. To live without Christ is to die without him. To die without him is to spend eternity without him. But if you want a life that satisfies, that has purpose and meaning, a life that demands the very best in you and, above all, a life that is pleasing to God – this is what God requires of you. Forgiveness and eternal life are not automatic; there is your part.

Something to admit
That you have sinned in the sight of God. Be deeply sorry for your sin. Hate it and be willing to turn from every thought, word, action and habit that you know to be wrong.

Something to believe
That Jesus Christ died on the cross bearing all the guilt and penalty of *your* sin.

Something to consider

That Jesus never promised it would be easy to follow him. Expect opposition, sneers and misunderstanding. Every part of your life, work, friendships, time, money, must all come under his control.

Something to do

Accept Jesus Christ into your life to be your Lord to control

you, your Saviour to cleanse you, your Friend to guide and be with you.

So many miss this last step and thus never come to *know* Jesus Christ. Perhaps no verse in the Bible makes this last step clearer than Revelation 3:20. Jesus is speaking,

'Behold I stand at the door and knock; if any one hears my voice and opens the door, I will come in to him....'

Jesus Christ waits outside the door of your life. He will not force his way in. He wants to be asked in. The handle is on the inside; only you can open the door. You become a true Christian when you open the door of your life to Jesus Christ and let him come in and live in your heart and life.

Have you ever taken this step? Perhaps you have never realised before that there was anything for you to do. You can be baptised, go to church, yes, even read the Bible and pray, and still leave Jesus Christ outside the door of your life. Face this question honestly.

Is Christ outside your life or inside? Will you let him in or keep him out? You cannot ignore Christ's invitation for ever. Time is fast running out.

But if you are ready thoughtfully to open the door of your life to Jesus Christ, then find a place where you can be quiet and alone.

Think of Christ's love for you: the cross, the shame and pain, his body nailed to the cross, his blood shed, all for you. Think of what he saves you from: eternal destruction, separation from God for ever, which is what hell is. Think of the shortness of this life: after death there will be no more opportunity to turn to Christ. It will be too late.

Think of Jesus Christ knocking now, asking to come into your life. You want him to come into your life, or perhaps you want to make sure he has come into your life. It might help you to say this prayer, phrase by phrase, quietly, thoughtfully, thinking carefully what you are saying, and what you are doing.

Lord Jesus Christ, I know I have sinned in my thoughts, words and actions.

There are so many good things I have not done. There are so many sinful things I have done.

I am sorry for my sins and turn from everything I know to be wrong.

You gave your life upon the cross for me. Gratefully I give my life back to you.

Now I ask you to come into my life.

Come in as my Saviour to cleanse me. Come in as my Lord to control me. And I will serve you all the remaining years of my life in complete obedience.

Amen

Christ in you

You have said this prayer and meant it. What you have said is a fact. You have asked Jesus Christ to come into your life and he has come. He now lives in your heart by his Holy Spirit.

Don't rely on your feelings; you may not feel any different at the moment. Trust his sure promises.

'If any one hears my voice and opens the door, I will come in to him....' (Revelation 3:20)

'He who believes has eternal life.' (John 6:47)

'I am with you always, to the close of the age.' (Matthew 28:20)

You are now a member of God's Kingdom, a child of God's family, part of his Body the Church – all who trust in Jesus, whatever their colour, background, or intellect.

The way ahead

You have begun the journey into life. You are now at the start of a new life. You have in Jesus Christ an all-powerful, ever-present Friend and Captain, but in Satan a cunning and strong enemy. So you need to grow strong as a Christian. You need food, air and exercise.

FOOD

The Bible is the Christian's food. It is a living book and through it God will speak to you. Read it every day.

AIR

Prayer is the Christian's air. Talk to Jesus Christ naturally as to a close friend, yet respectfully remembering who he is. Spend time alone with him daily.

EXERCISE

Worship

Join a local church at once. Never miss being with Christians in church on Sunday.

Witness

Tell one other person within the next 24 hours what you have done, that you have surrendered your life to Christ. Don't be ashamed to be known as a Christian at work and at home.

For further reading

BY THE SAME AUTHOR
The Way Ahead
Directions
Is God There?

ALSO AVAILABLE

A 25-minute video presentation adapted from this booklet, entitled *Journey into Life, the Video,* featuring Cliff Richard, available from Kingsway Publications Ltd.

FOR DAILY BIBLE READING NOTES
Scripture Union
207-209 Queensway
Bletchley
Milton Keynes
MK2 2EB
'Every Day with Jesus' Crusade for World Revival, Waverley Abbey House
Waverley Lane
Farnham
Surrey GU9 8EP

journey into Life

What is a Christian?

Should I become a Christian, and if so, how?

And what will happen if I don't?

Is there really such a thing as sin?

This booklet answers these vital questions simply
and clearly, and has already helped thousands to
start their 'journey of faith'.

Kingsway

ISBN 0-85476-769-X

9 780854 767694